Nick and Mutt hunt
backward and forward
through the pages of this
book, and discover the
wonders of the world.

Translated by Christopher Clark
Edited and adapted by Colin Clark

© 1990 HAPPY BOOKS, Milan, Italy
This 1990 edition published by
DERRYDALE Books, distributed by Outlet
Book Company, Inc., a Random House
Company, 225 Park Avenue South, New York,
New York 10003.
Printed and bound in Italy.
ISBN 0-517-05243-1
8 7 6 5 4 3 2 1

Emanuela Bussolati

My Picture Word Book of
People, Places
and Things

Illustrated by
Sabrina Orlando

Derrydale Books
New York

CONTENTS

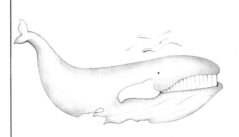

BEING BORN AND GROWING UP

 apple seed

 poppy seed

Everything that a plant needs to help it to develop is contained within its seed. Look at the apple and the poppy seeds.

Protected by the earth the seeds develop shoots that grow towards the light. Seedlings appear.

The poppy only grows for a single season. The apple tree grows year after year.

The hen keeps her eggs warm. Inside each egg a chick grows.

When the chicks are fully formed, they use their little beaks to break open the eggshells.

Some of the newly-hatched chicks will grow up to be roosters and some will grow into hens.

After a month the chicks have grown crests on their heads. It is still hard to tell male from female.

Now the chicks have grown up to become a rooster and a hen. Soon some eggs will be laid, and more chicks will be hatched.

The puppies are drinking milk from the mother dog. Puppies develop and grow very quickly.

At four months a puppy is independent, playful and curious. When he grows up, he will get together with a female, called a bitch, and more puppies will be born.

development is the changing of everything which grows.

Sow some seeds and watch the plants grow. See page 61.

When a woman and a man love each other, they can also become a mom and dad.

For nine months a baby develops inside its mother, protected in her womb.

A baby is born. It cries, drinks milk, and sleeps.

Make a book about yourself. How? See page 58.

At three months a baby can raise its head and smile.

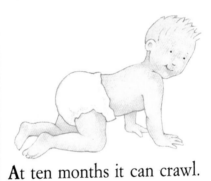

By six months baby can sit.

At ten months it can crawl.

At sixteen months it walks and says some words. At two years a child can draw.

At eight a child can dress himself. He can talk well and make up wonderful games.

The child continues to grow, and between twelve and sixteen the body changes again. The child becomes an adult. When a girl and a boy are older they may fall in love and marry.

SOME QUESTIONS ABOUT OUR BODIES

Why do we have bones? Just as the frame of a tent keeps it up, so our skeleton supports our body.

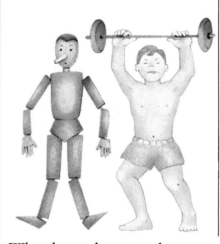

Why do we have tendons and muscles? To keep the parts of the skeleton together and enable us to move.

Why do we feel hot or cold? We feel things through the nerves which lie just under the skin. They tell the brain if something is hot or cold, wet, or dry.

If the nerves tell the brain that a flame burns, then the brain orders the muscles nearby to pull away.

Why do we get flushed? When we rush or feel happy or sad, the heart pumps more quickly and more blood flows under the skin.

What is a fever? It is the rise in body heat that occurs when the blood is fighting an infection.

How do we keep our balance? To make sure that a wall is perfectly upright and straight, a bricklayer uses a plumb line and a level. Something inside our ears works in the same way. When doing a somersault, our nerves tell the brain that we could fall over.

People wear all types of clothes. Look at page 22.

Infection: a cut that is inflamed and very painful has become infected.

Does unclean air harm us? When we breathe in we fill our lungs with air and the lungs filter out oxygen to keep our blood clean. Lungs cannot get oxygen from dirty air.

Why do we perspire when it is hot? Little drops of water, or perspiration, are pushed out to refresh the skin.

Why do we look like our parents? The first cell from which we developed had a "memory," just like a computer chip, which held many of our parents' features, and some were passed on to us.

What causes our skin color? It is caused by the mixing of melanine, which produces the dark color, and carotene, which is clear.

Where does food go when we eat it? It is changed in our stomachs and absorbed by the blood. The blood then passes it on to feed the cells in our body.

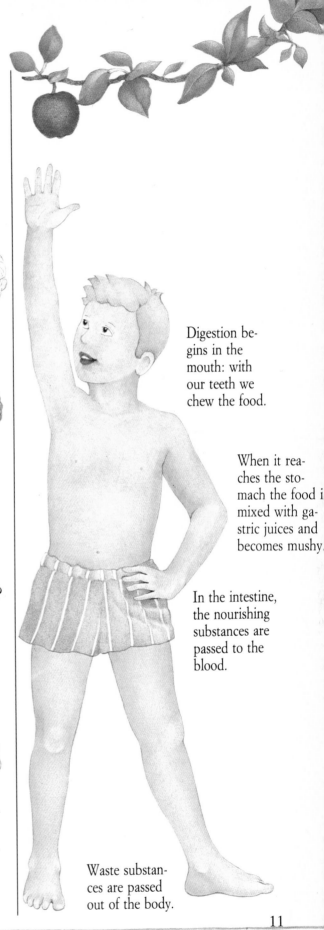

Digestion begins in the mouth: with our teeth we chew the food.

When it reaches the stomach the food i mixed with gastric juices and becomes mushy.

In the intestine, the nourishing substances are passed to the blood.

Waste substances are passed out of the body.

11

There are many ways to exercise. See pages 12 and 13.

What is good for us to eat? See pages 14 and 15.

LOTS OF DIFFERENT SPORTS

mountaineering

water-skiing

skiing

bobsledding

ice hockey

golf

judo

gymnastics

jogging

baseball

horse riding

12

Animals can set
records as well.
Turn to page
49.

hang-gliding

windsurfing

canoeing

sailing

swimming

soccer

tennis

cycling

fencing

There are people who hold records for running fastest and jumping highest, and performing the most daring acrobatics. People enjoy testing the limits of what their body can do. Sports, however, can help everyone stay healthy, even if they are only played for fun, and not for competition.

13

Have a "Funny Sports" Meeting with your friends. See page 58.

WHAT DO WE EAT?

All types of foods contain things that are good for us. These help us grow and give us energy. When our body needs food, we feel hungry, but it cannot tell us exactly what we should eat. We will only be healthy if we eat a variety of food; like meat, fish, fruit, and cheese. If we ate nothing except ice cream, we would no longer feel hungry, but our body would not be getting everything it needs to grow and be healthy.

Sugar makes food taste sweet and is a cause of decay in our teeth, so we must be sure to brush our teeth thoroughly after every meal.

An apple a day keeps the doctor away!... The peel and the fibers in an apple help our intestines digest all the food we eat.

If we want to have good eyesight we should eat lots of carrots and blackberries.

14

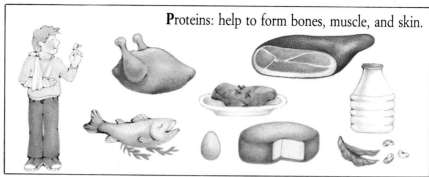
Proteins: help to form bones, muscle, and skin.

Carbohydrates: keep the body at the right temperature.

Fats: make energy and protect us from the cold.

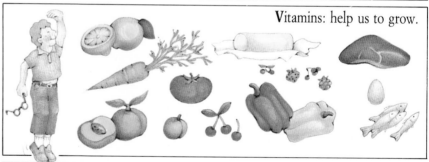
Vitamins: help us to grow.

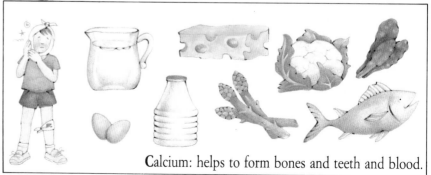
Calcium: helps to form bones and teeth and blood.

What is our nervous system for? See page 10.

People have invented many different ways of preserving food. Fruit, for example, can be made into jam.

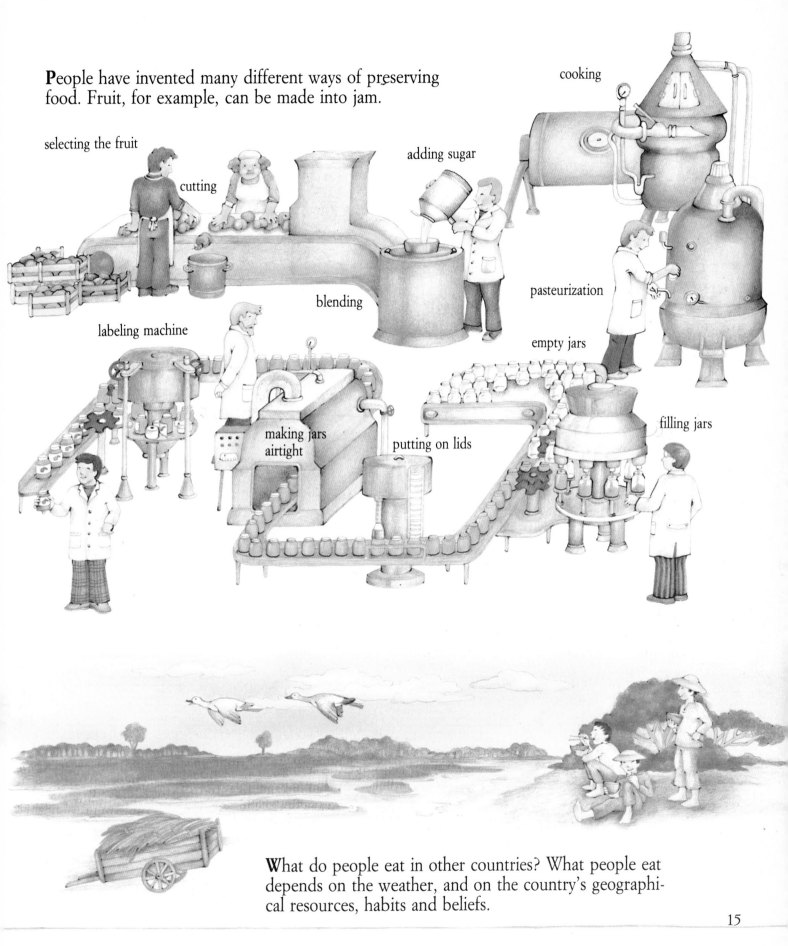

selecting the fruit

cutting

adding sugar

cooking

blending

pasteurization

labeling machine

empty jars

making jars airtight

putting on lids

filling jars

What do people eat in other countries? What people eat depends on the weather, and on the country's geographical resources, habits and beliefs.

15

Pasteurization
is a process of
heating liquids, to kill
harmful bacteria.

Make a meal
with your friends.
Turn to page
58 for a recipe.

FOOD AROUND THE WORLD

All over the world people work on the land, raising crops and animals for food. In some countries there is not enough for people to eat and in others there is too much. Often what is raised in one place is shipped great distances so others may eat it.

Poor countries do not have much to exchange or trade, and so they cannot buy all the food they need. People in many parts of the world suffer from poverty and hunger.

herring

salmon

oats

trout

wheat

canned fi

cod

dairy cattle

fruit

mackerel

sardines

citrus fruits

corn

eels

sardines

avocados

sugar cane

lobsters

anchovies

sweet potatoes

palm o

tuna

bananas

coconuts

shrimp

pineapples

sheep

manioc

cocoa

swordfish

beans

coffee

tomatoes

fruit

mackerel

beef cattle

tuna

manioc: a root from which a very nourishing flour is made.

herring

sheep

rye

barley

beer

pigs

wheat

potatoes

sunflower seeds

salmon

herring

potatoes

grapes

dairy cattle

sugar beets

caviar

sheep

rice

cheese

corn

sturgeon

sheep

farm animals

ed fish

fruit

sheep

citrus fruits

olives

grapes

horses

pigs

sardines

vegetables

almonds

citrus fruits

goats

cinnamon

poultry

figs

onions

rice

sesame seeds

dates

dates

tea

mangoes

millet

goats

pineapples

cocoa

tuna

squid

breadfruit trees

bananas

coffee

barracudas

peanuts

pepper

shrimp

fruit

cloves

shellfish

coconuts

sheep

mackerel

papayas

vanilla

sheep

sugar cane

mullet

wheat

sardines

krill

17

krill: tiny shellfish which live in the cold seas. Krill is a food for whales, and people.

How does food help us to stay healthy? See page 14.

MAN'S USE OF ANIMALS

The first men had to hunt animals in order to stay alive. They drew pictures of hunting on cave walls.

Shepherds learned to make use of more and more things from animals, like a sheep's wool.

To make luxury fur coats, we run the risk of making some animals extinct.

From buffalo, North American Indians got most things they needed to help them to stay alive; meat to eat, fur for clothes, bone for tools and arrowheads for weapons.

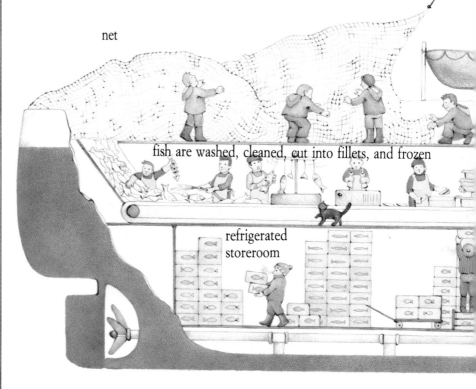

net

fish are washed, cleaned, cut into fillets, and frozen

refrigerated storeroom

How do we make use of animals for our clothing? Turn to page 22.

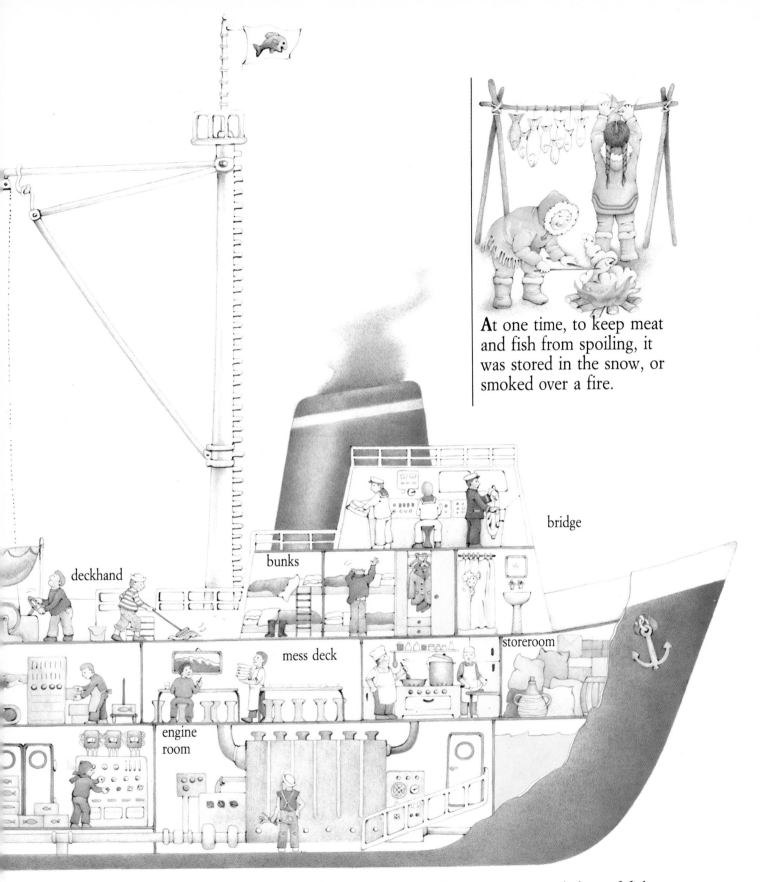

At one time, to keep meat and fish from spoiling, it was stored in the snow, or smoked over a fire.

bridge

deckhand

bunks

storeroom

mess deck

engine room

Today there are factory ships that can catch lots of fish, keep them from going bad and put them into packages.

19

On page 50 you can see animals in their natural environments.

ALL KINDS OF HOMES

cave

tent

stone house

raised hut

igloo

African house

pioneer's wagon

People have always built many different kinds of homes for themselves and their families. To protect themselves from weather, and from enemies, to store their belongings, and bring up their children in peace, they have found shelter in caves, built huts from bamboo, wood, or even mud; people have built houses of bricks and stones; homes have been built on stilts and on wheels.

Would you like to work with clay? Turn to page 59.

house in Pompeii

Pompeii: a Roman
city destroyed
by the eruption of
Mount Vesuvius in 79 A.D.

People work
and earn money
in many ways.
See page 56.

21

WAYS OF DRESSING

The wool for scarves comes from the fleece of sheep.

The fibers for a waterproof jacket are coated with oil.

Leather for our shoes comes from the hide of calves.

Clothes are made from many different kinds of material, both natural and man-made.

The material in our jeans is made from the fibers of the cotton plant.

pregnant woman

football player

astronaut   factory worker   gardener   monk   horserider   ballerina

Nigerian

Egyptian   Indian   Peruvian   Eskimo   Hawaiian   European

 bridesmaid

bride and groom

There are clothes made specially for every job and every sport, for all types of weather and for every occasion.

For a variety of sports clothes look at pages 12 and 13.

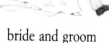

The seasons influence what we wear. Turn to page 38.

Prehistory

Ancient Egypt

Ancient Crete

Ancient Greece

Ancient Rome

Middle Ages: courtiers

Middle Ages: peasants

Middle Ages: Vikings

Renaissance

16th century

17th century

18th century

19th century: middle class family

19th century: Empire style

French Revolution

20th century: the Thirties

20th century: the Sixties

20th century: the Eighties

The way we dress has changed continuously throughout history. Each time has had its own styles and fashions.

23

You will find a Roman house on page 21.

DISCOVERING THE WORLD OF PLANTS

The plant kingdom is very large. Plants and flowers grow everywhere: in forests, arctic lands, deserts. Even on mountain tops there are plants that live by attaching themselves to the rocks.

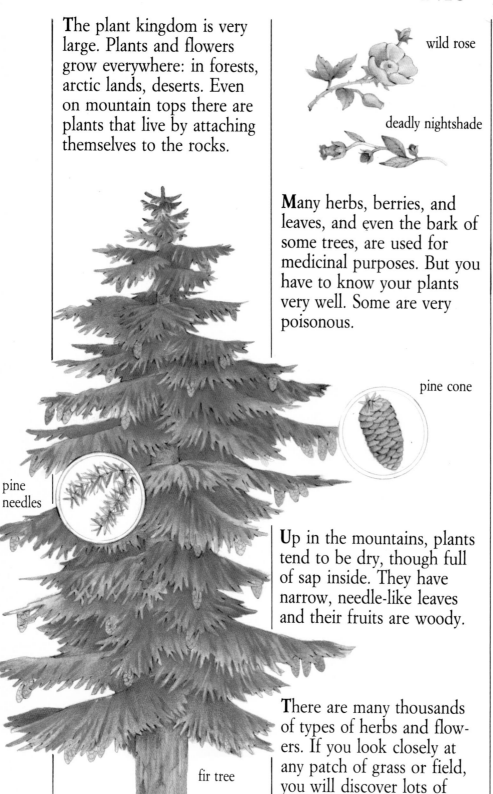
pine needles

pine cone

fir tree

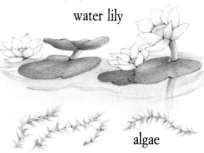
water lily

wild rose

deadly nightshade

algae

Many herbs, berries, and leaves, and even the bark of some trees, are used for medicinal purposes. But you have to know your plants very well. Some are very poisonous.

Up in the mountains, plants tend to be dry, though full of sap inside. They have narrow, needle-like leaves and their fruits are woody.

There are many thousands of types of herbs and flowers. If you look closely at any patch of grass or field, you will discover lots of different ones for yourself.

There are also plants that grow in water, in lakes, rivers, and seas. They are called aquatic plants.

bonsai tree

Plants come in all sorts of shapes and sizes, to fit and survive in their surroundings.

In the desert, plants are fat and fleshy. They have thorns instead of leaves to help to keep in water.

fatty plant

Linen for sheets, cotton for clothing, hemp for bags and rope: all these are woven out of threads obtained from the fibers or fruits of different plants.

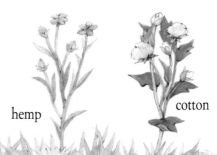
hemp

cotton

There are different types of environments on page 51.

Go collect herbs and leaves on page 61.

On page 60 you can find out how to tell the age of a tree.

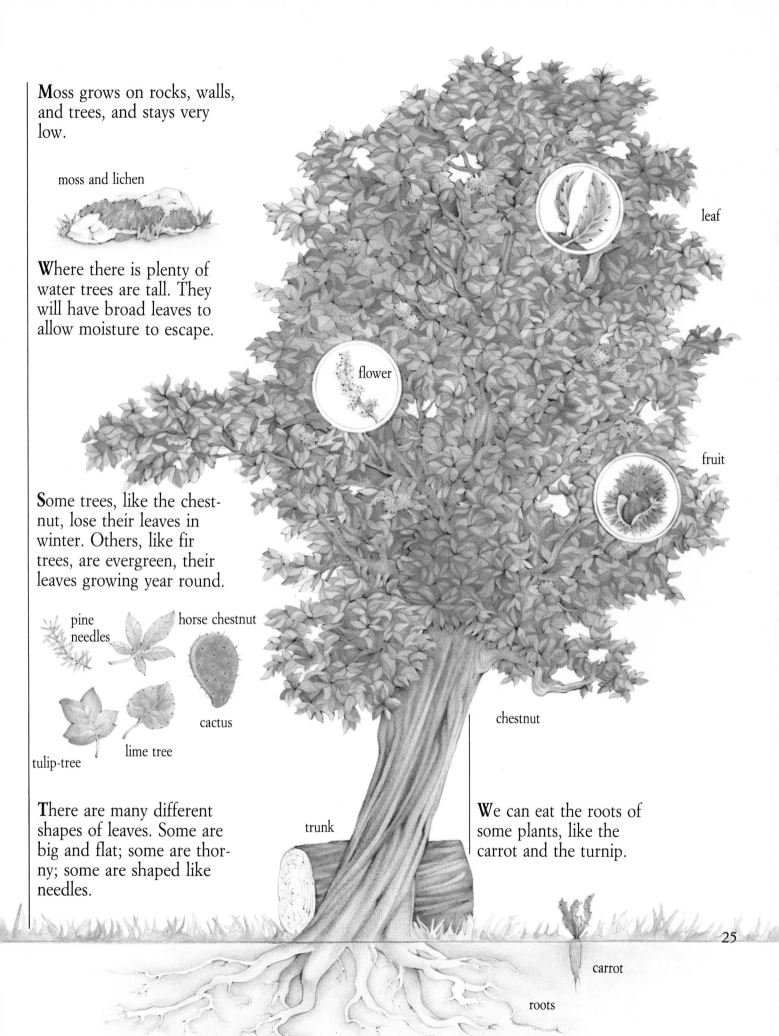

Moss grows on rocks, walls, and trees, and stays very low.

moss and lichen

Where there is plenty of water trees are tall. They will have broad leaves to allow moisture to escape.

Some trees, like the chestnut, lose their leaves in winter. Others, like fir trees, are evergreen, their leaves growing year round.

pine needles

horse chestnut

cactus

tulip-tree

lime tree

There are many different shapes of leaves. Some are big and flat; some are thorny; some are shaped like needles.

leaf

flower

fruit

chestnut

trunk

We can eat the roots of some plants, like the carrot and the turnip.

carrot

roots

25

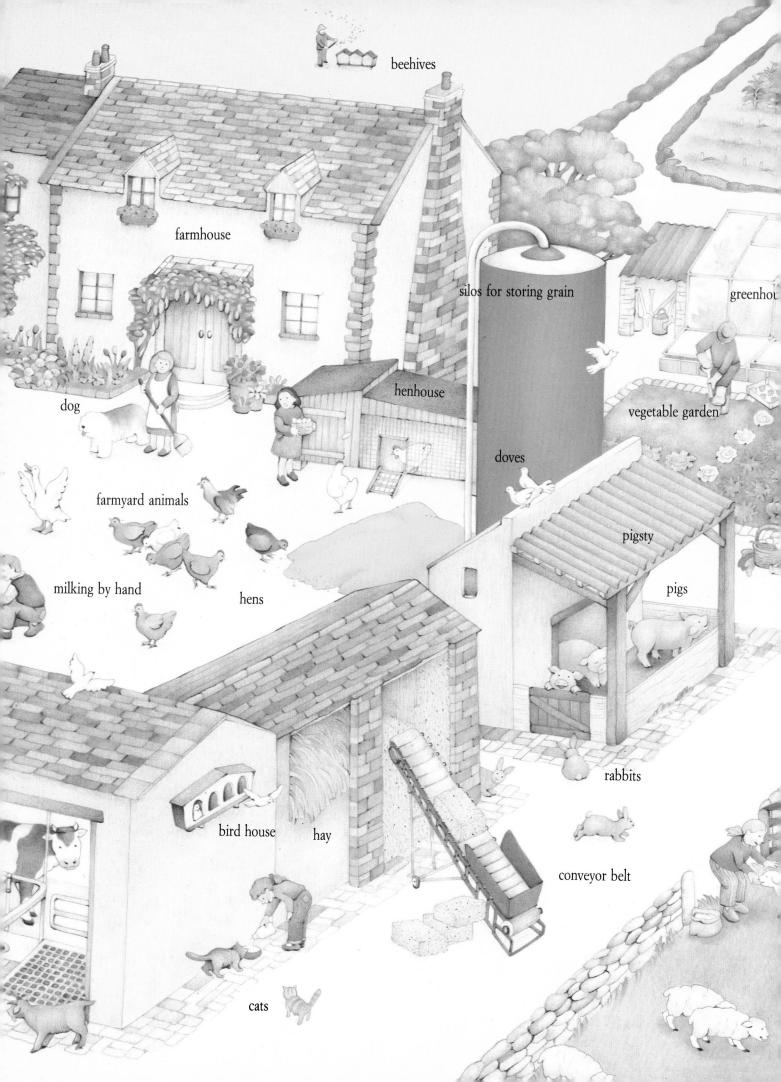

beehives

farmhouse

silos for storing grain

greenhou

dog

henhouse

vegetable garden

doves

farmyard animals

pigsty

pigs

milking by hand

hens

rabbits

bird house

hay

conveyor belt

cats

THE FARM

grazing land

stables

horse

geese

goats

cowshed

milk truck

mechanical milker

FARM ANIMALS

cow

goat

rooster, hen and chicks

ducks

sheep

horse

Find out how
to photograph
animals. See
page 59.

26

Open the page...

pig

doves

donkey

goose

rabbit and bunnies

turkey

cat

sheepdog

...and discover the farm!

ditch

orchard

picking fruit

cow and horse
manure make
the land fertile

tractor

grass cutter

A farm has just about everything we need to live. The milk from the cows and the goats is made into cheese, cream, and butter. Wool from the sheep and goats can be woven into clothes. The hens lay eggs, while rabbits, cattle, chickens and pigs are used for meat. In the fields, hay and oats are grown to feed the animals, while wheat, barley, fruit and vegetables are eaten by people. Each season has its harvest, and even in winter, thanks to greenhouses, there are many types of fruits and vegetables to eat, and everything can be sold for money to buy things which are not produced on the farm.

cornfield

combine harvester

water sprinkler

pumpkin field

sheep grazing

meadow

ANIMALS AS PETS

hamster

Never give a goldfish sugar or breadcrumbs to eat. Do not pour cold water into its bowl as the cold can kill it.

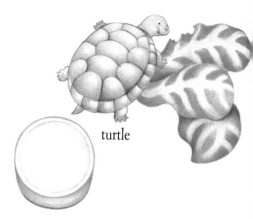

turtle

The hamster enjoys sunflower seeds and fruit. It stores food in its large cheek pouches.

From the huge Saint Bernard to the tiny Chihuahua, dogs are still the best friends for children.

goldfish

A turtle will be happy and healthy if you give it clean, fresh water and lots of fruit and vegetables.

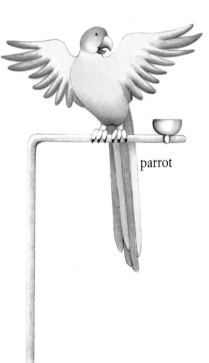

parrot

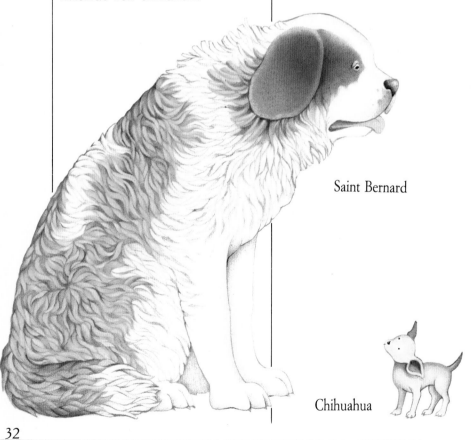

Saint Bernard

Chihuahua

To teach a parrot to say something, you must repeat the word to it, over and over again.

If you want to train a pet, page 59 will help you.

 birds

chipmunks

Wild birds will often come into your garden if you leave out food and water to attract them.

The only birds which should be kept in cages are those which are bred for the purpose.

Chipmunks make fun pets. They love to turn somersaults. They dig in the earth and enjoy apples and peanuts.

Cats are born hunters, but they learn quickly to behave well in the house, and they become good pets.

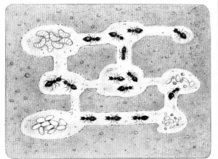

Keep a terrarium if you like reptiles or insects. Never leave the animals without plenty of food or water.

To make a terrarium, all you need is a container with earth, stones, and plants.

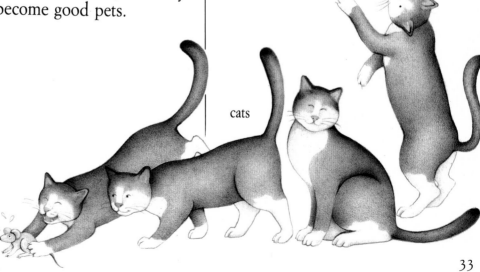
cats

Don't forget the things your pet needs. See page 59.

Bird feeders: places where you put out food and water for wild birds.

THE RIVER

The sun's heat makes the sea water turn into mist.

The mist rises and forms the clouds.

rain

snow

The clouds meet cold air and change into rain, sleet, or snow.

The rain that falls helps to fill the streams, rivers, and underground springs.

river

The rivers give us water to drink and wet our fields.

barge

tributary

Where the river is deep and wide enough, barges carry goods to different ports.

The river is fed by other smaller rivers, or, tributaries, until it flows into the sea.

boat

the sea

salmon

barbel

trout

carp

The water has to be pushed by pumps up to the highest floors of tall buildings.

The water from the river is purified, or cleaned, before we can use it in the city.

tower for drinking water

purifier

water truck

pump

After it has been used, water passes down drains into the sewage system.

drain for sewer

purifier

filter

Because dirty water causes pollution, water is again purified before it is put back in the river or sea.

35

pike

catfish

sturgeon

THE SEA

Streams of water, called currents, cross oceans and move warm or cold water from one part to another.

The oceans and seas cover most of the surface of our planet, the Earth.

The water in the seas and oceans never stops moving: waves of all sizes are made by the force of the wind.

Twice each day the tide makes the level of the sea rise and fall again.

boats

rocks

bay

gulf

inlet

promontory

peninsula

sailboat

windsurfing

shoals of sand

ship

lighthouse

man-made harbor

canal

36

cuttle-fish

lobster

dory

jellyfish

Moray eel

fish farm

helicopter

trench

oil-drilling
platform

The sea is very important
as a source of food: we
catch fish in the open sea
and breed fish and
shell-fish along the coast.

The sea's color depends on
its depth and the color of
the sky above it.

flying fish

dolphins

fishing boat

Special platforms are built
to drill into the sea floor
searching for minerals or oil
or gas.

Millions of plants and animals live in the sea.

island

seagulls

The sea floor is very varied:
it has flat areas, mountains,
deep valleys and volcanoes.

Along the coast, men also
create large basins where
sea-water turns into mist
and salt is left behind.

rocky coast

salt works

lagoon

37

remora

shark

mackerel

moon-fish

Manta ray

FINDING OUT ABOUT NATURAL EVENTS

Why is there night and day? Push a fork into an apple, and keep the fork at the same angle as you use it to roll the apple around a table lamp.

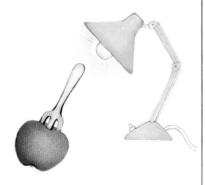

As the apple rolls around the lamp, only half of it faces the light. The two halves keep changing places.

The apple is the Earth, the lamp is the Sun. In 24 hours the Earth turns once on its axis, and we pass from day to night, and back.

In the spring, the sun warms the air. Days become lighter. On the other side of the world it is fall. The days there become cooler and shorter.

In the summer it is very hot and the days are longer than the nights. On the other side of the world it is winter. The days are shorter than the nights and it is cold.

What is climate? It is the weather condition of an area, determined by the seasons, the sun and the surroundings.

axis of rotation: the imaginary point around which the Earth turns.

steam: the little cloud of mist which forms above boiling liquids.

How are clouds formed? If you heat a pot of water, after a while steam will come out of it. Some of the water has turned into steam.

Under the sun's heat some of the Earth's water turns into gas or mist and gathers together to form clouds.

Why does it rain? Some of the mist in the clouds turns back into drops of water, they join together, become heavy, and rain falls.

What is a rainbow? Light is made up of many colors that we cannot usually see. When light shines through rainwater at an angle it is split up into these colors and we see the rainbow.

What are hailstones? Each one is a drop of water that has been covered by layers of ice in the cold air.

Why does it snow? When the air is very cold, small "crystals" of ice are formed which stick to each other, falling as snow.

Why does everything fall to Earth? Because the Earth is so large, it acts like a magnet, attracting everything nearby. Something seems heavy because the Earth pulls it with its "force": this force is gravity.

People on the other side of the world do not feel upside down. Thanks to gravity everyone is the right way up if their feet are on the ground!

What is wind? It is the air moving from cold to warm parts of the world, like the breeze that comes when you open a window in a room.

What is lightning? Drops of rain collide in clouds, causing electricity, which sparks as a lightning flash.

What is thunder? Because a lightning flash is very hot it heats the air so fast that it expands with an explosion.

39

Make a rainbow. Follow the directions on page 60.

Discover the wonders of snowflakes. See page 60.

THE PLANET EARTH

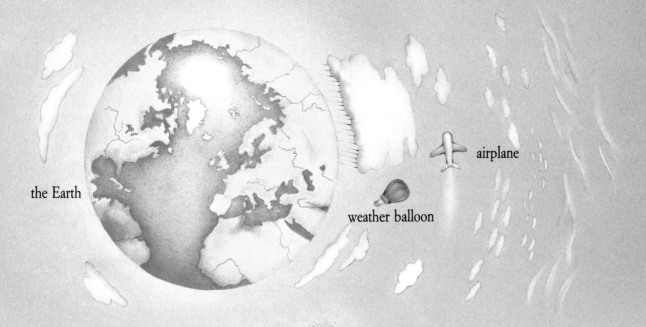

the Earth

airplane

weather balloon

The great ball that is the Earth has a solid core with melted rock around it and a cold crust on the surface.

The atmosphere, a layer of air, separates Earth from space. This layer keeps out too much heat from the sun, but allows enough for life to grow.

Melted rock, or "magma," is held in by the crust. If the crust breaks, the melted rock bursts out from a volcano.

When parts of the crust move and rub together, earthquakes may occur.

Over hundreds of years, the wind can shape, and change the form of rocks.

Seas and rivers smooth rocks and stones, changing the shape of the landscape.

40

atmosphere: the layer of gas surrounding planets and stars.

Make your own mineral collection. See page 60.

shooting stars

spacecraft

the Moon

The Earth has a "satellite," the Moon, which moves around it. Earth and Moon move around the Sun together.

The Moon is held in place by the pull of the Earth's gravity, but it also uses its own pull on the Earth.

Large areas of water, like the oceans, move and change because of the gravitational pull of the Moon.

By the seashore, you can see the ocean come in and go out twice a day. Called the tide, this motion is caused by the pull of the Moon, and also by the Sun.

41

force of gravity: the pull which is used by a large object in space.

THE UNIVERSE

Long ago, people thought that the sky was a round ceiling filled with stars, hanging over the earth.

After Galileo made the first telescope it was easier to look at the sky and have a clear idea of the stars and planets.

We now know that our "Solar System" is only a tiny part of the "universe."

Our Solar System is made up of the planets, including Earth, and the star we call the Sun, and, with 400 billion other stars, is part of a giant galaxy.

On a clear, starry night you can see the galaxy in which the Earth moves-it is called the Milky Way.

9 planets, 43 satellites, comets, asteroids and millions of meteorites all revolve around the Sun.

Find out on page 60 how some of the stars were given names.

If you have come from outer space, pages 34 to 41 tell you about Earth!

The ancient Greeks named the planets that they could see after their gods: Mercury, Venus, Mars, Jupiter and Saturn. Uranus, Neptune and Pluto were not discovered until later.

Dictionary of the sky

Asteroids: hundreds of pieces of rock which revolve around the Sun between Mars and Jupiter.

Galaxy: a large group of stars.

Meteorites: natural rocks or metal pieces reaching Earth from space.

Planet: a solid, round body, like the Earth, which revolves around a star, like the Sun, and receives light from it.

Satellite: an object, like the Moon, revolving around a planet.

Solar System: a group of planets, satellites, and asteroids that revolve around the Sun.

Star: a natural body in space producing its own light, like the Sun.

the Sun

Mercury   Venus   Earth   Mars   Jupiter   Saturn   Uranus   Neptune   Pluto

43

Do you know the signs of the Zodiac? They are explained on page 60.

HOW LIFE BEGAN ON EARTH

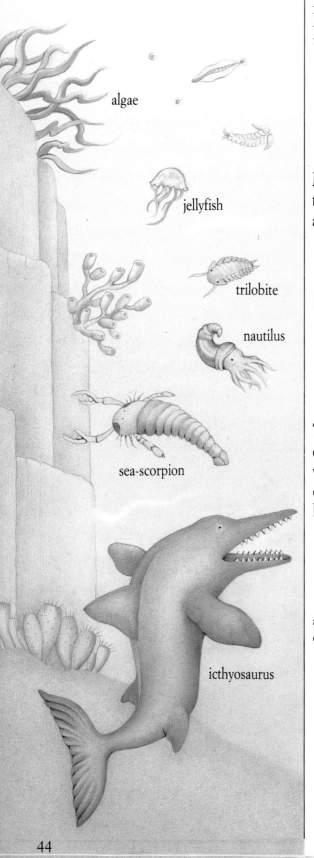

algae

jellyfish

trilobite

nautilus

sea-scorpion

icthyosaurus

In all its forms, life on Earth had its beginning in the sea.

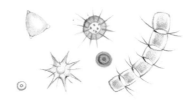

Many millions of years ago, the first simple plants and animals were formed.

jellyfish

The first creatures to come out of the sea were the "invertebrates." Like jellyfish or snails, they had no bones.

anatosaurus
duck-billed dinosaur

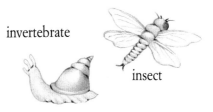

invertebrate

insect

Then came plants on dry land, insects, invertebrates and amphibians.

primitive reptile

The first animals with back-bones, or "vertebrates" were reptiles, who were able to move about with ease on strong legs.

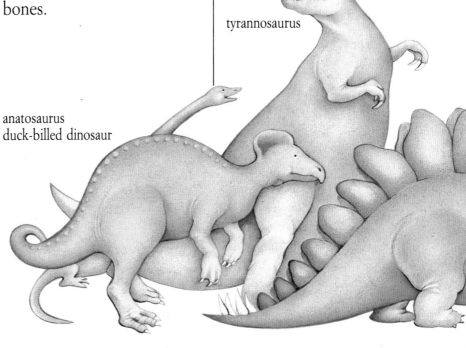

tyrannosaurus

On page 61 you can find out about dinosaur records.

Turn the page and you will see some of the relatives of prehistoric animals.

pteranodon

Dinosaurs appeared about 205 million years ago. The continents then formed two huge land areas – Europe, North America and Asia to the north, Africa and South America to the south.

Before the first men had appeared, about 65 million years ago, the dinosaurs suddenly ceased to exist.

mammoth

saber-toothed tiger

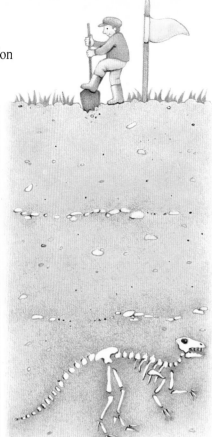

The climate was hot and wet and the land covered in forest.

Over millions of years, some reptiles changed into mammals. Female mammals give birth and nurse them. Humans are highly-developed mammals.

By digging in sandy soil, people have found the skeletons of many dinosaurs. From these we can discover the different sizes and shapes of these strange creatures.

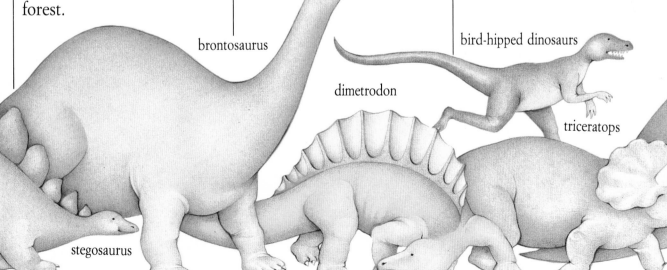
brontosaurus

dimetrodon

bird-hipped dinosaurs

triceratops

stegosaurus

fossils: the trace of something that lived a long time ago, preserved in rocks.

DIFFERENT KINDS OF ANIMALS

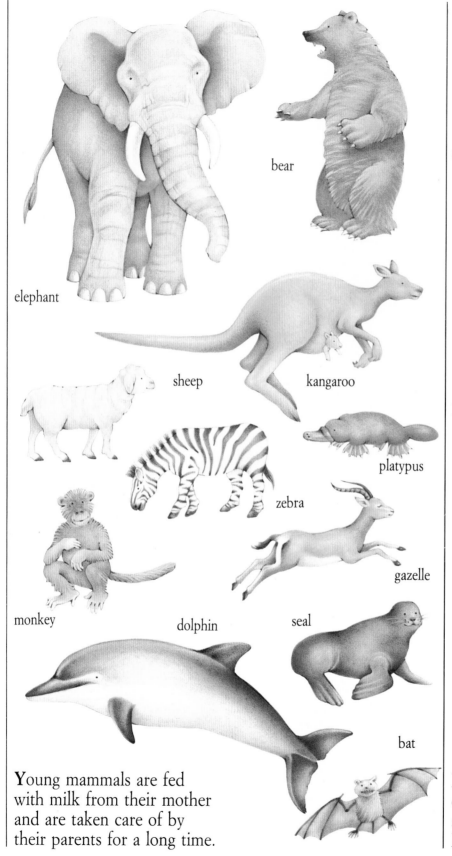

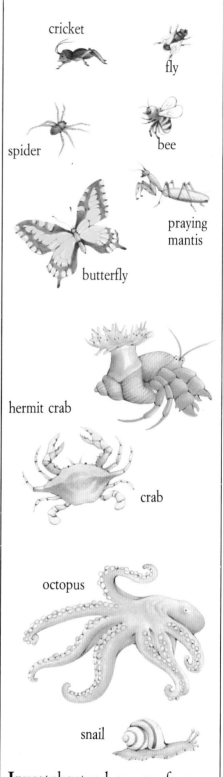

elephant

bear

sheep

kangaroo

zebra

platypus

monkey

gazelle

dolphin

seal

bat

cricket

fly

spider

bee

butterfly

praying mantis

hermit crab

crab

octopus

snail

Young mammals are fed with milk from their mother and are taken care of by their parents for a long time.

Invertebrates have no frame of bones, or skeleton; some are covered by a hard shell, like the crab.

Why are some animals in danger of extinction? See page 61.

hummingbird

seagull

swallow

goose

pelican

flamingo

penguin

condor

A bird's body is covered by feathers. The front limbs are called wings. The young birds hatch from eggs.

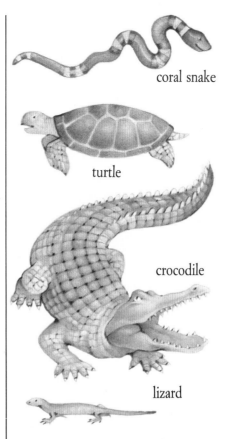

coral snake

turtle

crocodile

lizard

Reptiles are cold-blooded animals whose bodies are covered in scales. They lay their eggs on dry land.

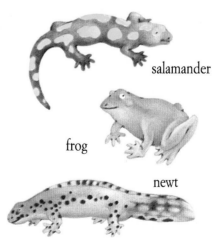

salamander

frog

newt

Amphibians live both on land and in water. As they grow up their bodies change completely.

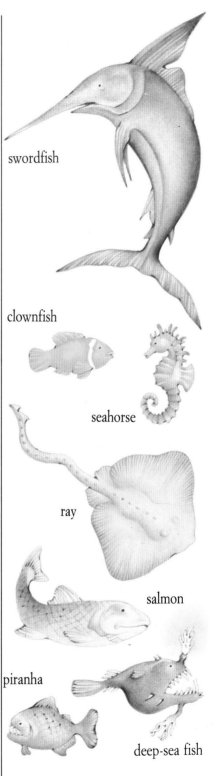

swordfish

clownfish

seahorse

ray

salmon

piranha

deep-sea fish

Fish have cold blood and breathe through "gills." They use their fins and tail for moving in the water.

From pages 26 to 31, we show you people working with animals.

ANIMALS AS FRIENDS

Sled dog

ox

camel

horse

donkey

sea hawk

seeing-eye dog

hamster

People work with many animals. They use the natural abilities of some: cats to catch mice, birds to catch fish. They benefit from the strength of others: the elephant can lift great weights; the horse can carry us from one place to another; and the donkey can quietly carry a heavy load. We eat and drink the produce of other animals, like the eggs from a hen or the milk from a cow.

And, of course, we love small animals just for their friendship and love: dogs, cats, hamsters and birds.

Which animals do people like to keep as pets? See pages 32 and 33.

Animals are also valuable on farms. Turn back to page 27.

seal

puffin

geese

lemming

stork

reindeer

Arctic fox

moose

panda

fox

brown bear

badger

wild boar

leopard

elephant

tuna

camel

swallows

zebra

crocodile

buffalo

tiger

gazelle

giraffe

elephant

orangutan

monkey

lion

hippopotamus

koala bear

kangaroo

rhinoceros

shark

monitor lizard

...and discover where animals live.

camels

giraffe

lion

zebras

snake

kangaroos

fennec

kiwi

scorpion

duck-billed platypus

The few trees survive water shortages by storing water during the rains that flood huge areas twice each year.

Since scarce water would dry up on leaves, desert plants have spines and thorns that hold water.

Australia is a vast island. The wild life in its deserts, forests and grasslands is very different.

TROPICAL FORESTS

SAVANNAH

toucan

parrot

orangutan

elephant

gorilla

tiger

snake

panther

crane

rhinoceros

gazelle

hippopotamus

In the tropical forests, of Asia, Africa and South America, there is constant heat and the air is full of mist. Trees reach great heights and all kinds of flowers, fruits, vines, and plants grow.

In a zone which is very hot by day and very cold at night, the savannah is like an enormous meadow.

PEOPLE AT WORK

teacher   pupils   caretaker

baker   news reporter   sailor   painter   forestry worker   billboard man

scientist   bricklayer   fashion designer   butcher   TV cameraman   TV host

Lots of different people work, so that we can have food to eat, stay healthy, travel, and enjoy ourselves.

To work more quickly and easily, people have invented many different forms of transportation and many complicated machines.

Many inventions help us to live well and longer. Others are designed to answer our questions, about the world in which we live.

dentist   dental technician

sick animals   veterinarian

You have to wear special clothes to do some work. See page 22.

ON THE MOVE

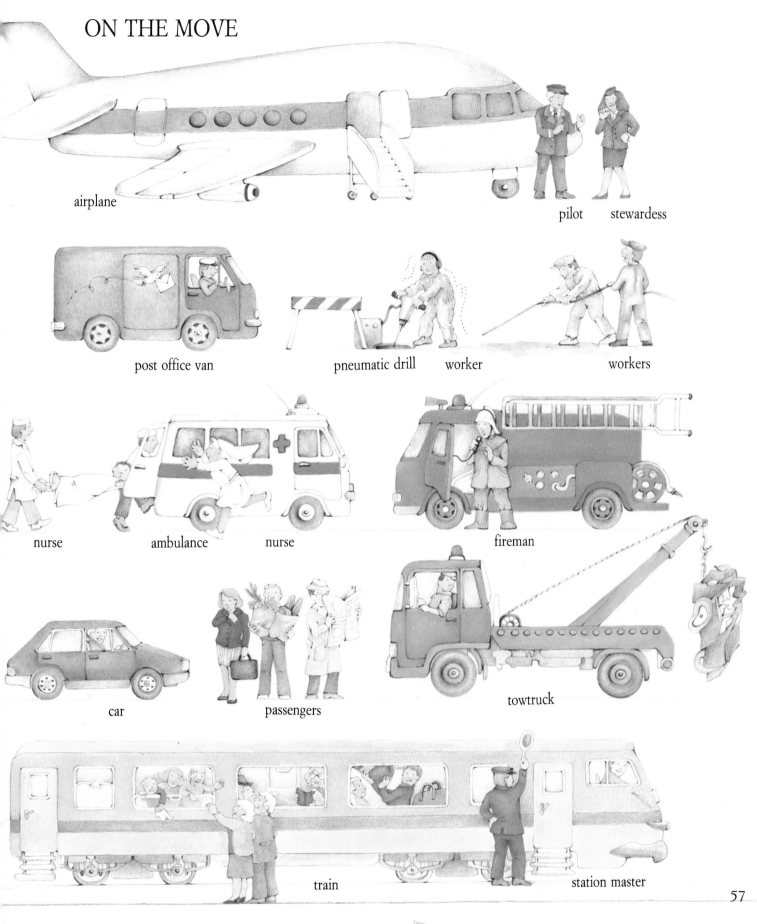

airplane

pilot stewardess

post office van

pneumatic drill worker workers

nurse ambulance nurse

fireman

car passengers

towtruck

train station master

LOTS OF THINGS TO DO, LOTS OF THINGS TO KNOW

Tell the story of yourself

Do you like looking at photos of yourself when you were young and hearing about the things you did? If you do, why not make up a book about yourself, telling your very own story. Here's how to do it. Collect your favorite photos of yourself and ask your parents if they still have any of your old baby clothes and make photocopies of them. Then interview your relatives. Ask them to tell you stories about some of the funny things that you did when you were little.

Then get a photo album, a pair of scissors, a tube of glue and some colored pencils. Glue all the pictures that you have into the album, and write down your own memories, plus the stories you have been told. Put the title on the cover: 'My Story' by 'Me'!

A "Funny Sports" Meeting

Taking part in some kind of sport is a great way of keeping in shape. Here are some ideas for a *funny sports* meet that you can organize with your friends.
– Running a race while holding a ping pong ball in a spoon. Next hold the other end of the spoon in your mouth!
– Walking around for three minutes with a book balanced on your head.
– Crawling under a line of low chairs, without moving any of them.
Of course, there are many more interesting events.

These might prove more difficult!
– Unwrap three chocolates in one minute, wearing thick ski gloves.
– Try and take a bite out of an apple on the end of a string, without using your hands. Who is going to be the winner of these events?

An unusual recipe

Although it is not at all unusual nowadays for us to eat potatoes and tomatoes, these actually were brought from South America hundreds of years ago. If your friends do not think that there is anything special about them, try them with this dish. You will need:
3 1/2 ounces of boiled rice
2 bananas
1 avocado pear
1/2 can of sliced pineapples

plus some raisins, mustard, oil and vinegar, salt and pepper.
Soak the raisins in water for 20 minutes. Ask an adult to cut up the bananas, avocado and pineapple. Add the raisins and the fruit to the rice.
For extra flavor, add some oil, vinegar, salt and pepper, and a little mustard. Serve this dish cold. You will find that it is a great success.

Working with clay

The first bricks ever made by men in ancient times were of clay. Naturally, clay is found on the bottoms of rivers, but you can get it more easily in a store. Here are some suggestions on working with clay, just as men did in olden times, and how to make some things for yourself. Always keep your clay damp and only work with a small amount at a time. Knead it and beat it to remove the air bubbles. Then flatten the clay with a rolling pin. Divide it and make up a lot of rectangular bricks. When they are dry, you can use these bricks to build miniature houses.

You can also make a dish out of clay. Squeeze the clay into a ball and dig out the middle, then smooth it around the edge. When it is dry, you can use this dish to keep things in, like coins, or paper clips.

A reminder bulletin board for your pets

Here is an idea to help you look after your pets. Get a piece of cardboard and glue a photo of your pet on the top left-hand corner. On the right, stick a piece of paper for making notes: Food, Buy, Vet, Medicine, etc. Make a hole at the bottom of the board. Tie some string through the hole and tie a pencil to the other end. Then you will always have it there ready for you to write down everything you must remember.

How to photograph your pet

If you follow these hints, you can take pictures of your pet in all sorts of different poses. Be sure to photograph your pet in a place that is well lit and has no shadows. If your pet is large, stand at least five steps away when taking a picture. If the pet is small, two steps will be enough.

How to train your pet properly

Pets are usually very trusting of people and easy to train. But you need lots of patience and you have to study animal behavior. Move slowly and use only a few words so that the animal begins to understand your language. Only teach your animal to do one thing at a time, alternating lessons with rest periods. In this way you can teach a dog to bring you things, or a parrot to talk, or a hamster to come into your hand without being afraid. Always remember to reward your pet for his efforts, with food, kind words, and petting. If he makes a mistake, just say "no" in a firm voice, and keep repeating the exercise patiently. If you continue to have patience yourself and show kindness at all times, you will find that you can teach your pet to listen.

Look and learn

If you have the desire to learn, a few simple instruments and a good eye, then you can discover so many things. For example, have you ever looked at a snowflake through a magnifying glass? You will see that a snowflake is a perfect crystal, and each flake is different from all the others. What shape is a dewdrop? Look for yourself and find out. Did you know that if you spray water from a hose with the sun behind you, you can make your own rainbow? What do you discover when you look at a blade of grass through a microscope? Although, to the naked eye, the grass looks smooth, it is really covered by small hairs and veins.

If you look at the Moon through a strong telescope, what will you discover? The face of the Moon is a mass of "craters" or holes, large and small.

The signs of the Zodiac

Do you know if you are a Leo or an Aquarius? Are you a Virgo or a Scorpio? The signs of the Zodiac are the "constellations," or groups of stars, that the Sun "visits" during the year, although it is actually the Earth that moves, not the Sun. Your sign is the constellation which the Sun was "visiting" at the time of your birth. As the Earth spins at a regular speed, the Sun "visits" the same constellation at the same time each year.

Every star has a story

In ancient times, men named the stars and constellations after the gods who could be found in their myths and legends. Orion, for example, was a proud hunter. He was killed by Artemis, the goddess of hunting, because she caught him spying on her. Zeus, the king of the gods, changed him into a constellation. And so, even now, on summer nights we can look up at the stars of Orion.

Collecting minerals

Water, rain, wind, and earthquakes all change the landscape. If you look carefully at rocks and stones you can see the changes they have gone through. There are round stones which have been smoothed by water in the sea or in rivers. There are rocks with holes like sponges that were formed by fire, found near volcanoes. If you want to start your own collection of rocks and minerals, you should put each of your samples on trays with a sticker beside each. The sticker should state the date and place where you found it.

How to tell the age of a tree

Trees develop light, colored wood in the spring and darker wood in the winter. This can be seen in the freshly-cut surface of a tree trunk as a series of light and dark rings. The rings are smallest in the middle when the tree was young, and the most recent are at the edge. Count the light or dark rings to see how old the tree was.

A herbarium

A herbarium is a collection of preserved herbs, flowers and leaves. Why not make one of your own?
Place freshly gathered leaves and flowers between sheets of tissue paper. The samples must not touch each other. Put them under a pile of books for a week. When they are dry, glue them onto cardboard. Beside each item in your collection you should write down the date and place where you found it. You can learn the names of all your samples with the help of a manual or guide which you can buy in any good bookstore.

Sowing, growing and harvesting your own food

Have you ever felt that you would like to try growing something good to eat? It's easy. You can buy seeds for wheat, watercress, and soy, from a gardening shop. Get some wood charcoal from a fireplace or a barbecue. Put some cotton on a plate, then place a piece of charcoal on it. Wet the cotton with a little water. Wash

the seeds and put them on the plates also. Keep the plates in the dark for a few days. Wet the cotton from time to time. As soon as the seeds begin to sprout, put the plates out in the sunlight beside a window. When the shoots reach a height of about one inch, cut them. You can eat the shoots you have grown in a salad or on buttered bread.

Dinosaur records

It probably does not surprise you to learn that the dinosaurs were often very special record-breakers...
For example, one kind of marine reptile kept seventeen pounds of stones in its stomach. These stones crushed the food so it was easily digested. The pteranodon looked like a flying dragon, and had a wingspan that was as wide as six children all holding out their arms.
The tyrannosaurus was as tall as a giraffe, over nineteen feet. On the other hand, the earliest ancestor of the horse, the eohippus, was no bigger than a fox.

Why are some animals in danger of extinction?

You are certainly aware, that today many animals are in danger of extinction, due to man's use and abuse of his environment and surroundings.
The destruction of whole forests has upset the fragile balance of nature, just as fashion and fur coats have caused the death of millions of animals.
Sea, air and land pollution have equally contributed in creating difficult living conditions for all animals, including man. Fortunately many people today fight hard to protect nature and save endangered species. Areas have been set up to re-establish more harmonic living habitats amd many others where hunting has been forbidden.
We should all remind ourselves that the world is our precious home and become more and more aware of how we can help it change for the better with our love and respect.